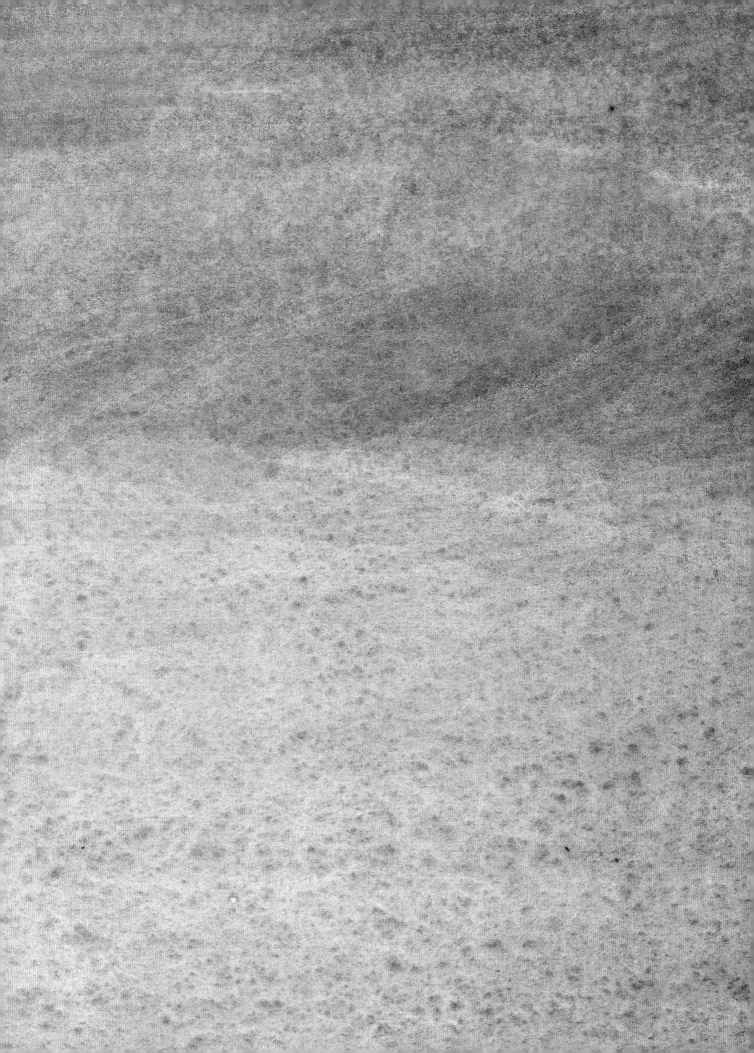

For all those people working to reduce the burning
of fossil fuels and keep the bears on ice
— B. Z. G.

For Anya
— I. S.

Many thanks to Laura Godwin, Reka Simonsen, Patrick Collins,
and all the others at Holt who helped with this book.

**SQUARE
FISH**

An Imprint of Macmillan
175 Fifth Avenue
New York, NY 10010
mackids.com

Square Fish and the Square Fish logo are trademarks of Macmillan and
are used by Henry Holt and Company under license from Macmillan.

Square Fish books may be purchased for business or promotional use.
For information on bulk purchases, please contact
the Macmillan Corporate and Premium Sales Department at
(800) 221-7945 x 5442 or by e-mail at specialmarkets@macmillan.com.

Library of Congress Cataloging-in-Publication Data
Guiberson, Brenda Z.
Ice bears / Brenda Z. Guiberson ; illustrated by Ilya Spirin.
p.   cm.
ISBN 978-1-250-04061-9
1. Polar bear—Arctic regions—Juvenile literature. 2. Parental behavior in animals—
Arctic regions—Juvenile literature. I. Spirin, Ilya, ill. II. Title.
QL737.C27G83 2008   599.786—dc22   2007040895

Originally published in the United States by Henry Holt and Company
First Square Fish Edition 2014
Book designed by Patrick Collins
Square Fish logo designed by Filomena Tuosto
The artist used watercolors on Arches watercolor paper
to create the illustrations for this book.

1 3 5 7 9 10 8 6 4 2

AR: 4.1 / LEXILE: AD860L

ICE
BEARS

Brenda Z. Guiberson

illustrated by

Ilya Spirin

 SQUARE FISH ✦ Henry Holt and Company ✦ New York

Winter is coming to the arctic. A female polar bear now has a body that jiggles like jelly. She has doubled her weight to a blubbery 800 pounds. She does not follow other polar bears onto the sea ice to hunt seals. Instead, she digs out a nesting den in a snowdrift. *Twishtwish.* Her extra fat will feed her as she spends the long, dark months ahead under the snow.

On a frigid December day, her cubs are born deaf, blind, and almost hairless. Each weighs barely a pound and is helpless to survive the blizzard outside—it is minus 50 degrees Fahrenheit! But the den is 30 degrees warmer, and the mother snuggles the twins into her rolls of insulating fur. *Slurpslurp.* She nurses them often. As she loses weight, they grow plump on her rich, creamy milk that is 30 percent fat.

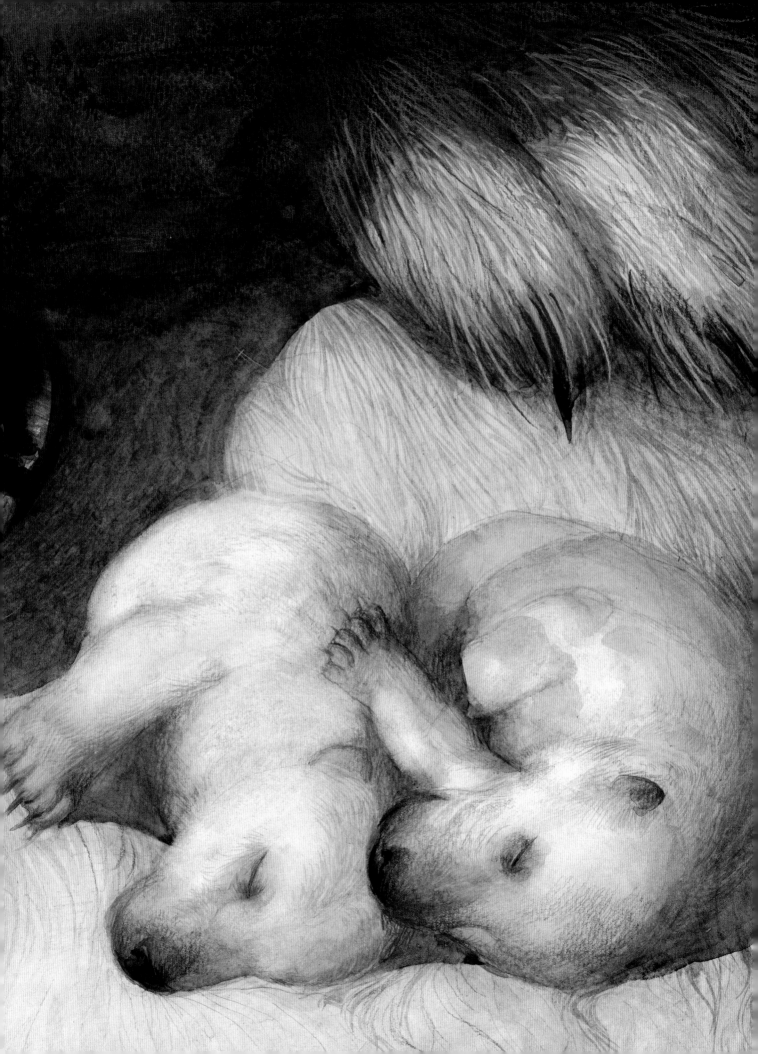

In March the mother bear senses the return of daylight. The extra pounds are gone, and her milk is thin. If she doesn't eat soon, none of them will survive. She digs out of the snow den and calls for her 20-pound cubs to follow.

The cubs blink at the bright sunlight and yelp at the far-off musk oxen. They huddle behind their mother when a white ptarmigan scoots by, camouflaged like the cubs against the snow. The bird has long feathers on its feet and glides over the snow—*shwoo, shwoo*—as if it is wearing snowshoes.

The mother gnaws on grass to get her stomach working again. She can smell ringed seals in the ocean 10 miles away, but the cubs are not yet strong enough to travel. And they have lessons to learn about survival in the arctic.

When she rolls in the snow to clean her fur, the cubs roll, too. When she digs into the snow to get out of the wind, they dig. When she sniffs the air, they sniff.

The mother smells wolves. She hustles her cubs into the den and blocks the entrance until the danger is gone.

On sunny days the polar bears are outside. The cubs tumble and roll. The mother shows them how to use their sharp claws and furry paws to keep from slipping. *Chuffchuff!*—she scolds when they wander too far. Finally, after two weeks of school, the mother slides with them all the way down the hill, and they head off toward the frozen ocean.

Day after day, the cubs struggle over the snow. They nurse and sleep often and ride piggyback when they are tired. At the edge of the sea ice, they are afraid of the grinding noises and strange smells, but the hungry mother urges them along. She is searching for a hole where seals pop up for a breath of air.

A male polar bear crosses their path. *Chuffchuff!* The mother orders the cubs behind her, then rears up on her hind legs. *Whap!* She swings at the male, who might kill her cubs if he gets close enough. He moves on.

The cubs trail after their mother. A fluffy white fox and two ravens follow them. When the mother stops, they all stop. She hisses until the cubs hold as still as a clump of ice. Then she crouches low over a breathing hole and does not move for a whole hour.

Gurgle . . . splosh! Finally a ringed seal pops up for a gulp of air. *Swoop!* The mother grabs it and devours the blubber. Then the cubs try the new food. As the bears leave, the arctic fox darts in for leftovers, and the ravens peck until the bones are clean.

The mother shows the cubs how she pounces through the snow to catch a baby seal. Every few days she must catch another seal to keep her milk flowing rich and creamy. After eating, the cubs wrestle, but the day is 20 degrees Fahrenheit, and they overheat quickly. They gobble snow to cool down as a long line of caribou crosses the tundra.

Twe twe twe! Honk! Honk! Quaaack! Great flocks of birds fly in for a short nesting season. The ones that arrive with extra fat are lucky, because on the snowy tundra there is not yet much for them to eat.

In June, with the sun in the sky both day and night, the arctic starts to thaw. As the sea ice thins, the mother bear searches even harder for seals. If she and the cubs don't pack on enough extra fat, they could starve to death by fall.

The deep ground, called permafrost, stays frozen solid, but the surface snow and ice melt. *Drip . . . drip . . . dribble!* Billions of mosquito eggs thaw. Bumblebee queens, the only bees to survive the winter, awaken. Lemmings swarm out from their crumbling snow tunnels. Plants poke through the softening snow already blooming for the short summer season.

KeeRAACK! The frozen ocean fractures into pieces. The mother and her cubs are caught on unstable ice in the middle of the break up. *Crunch, crick!* A cub gets his paw caught in a crack. The mother struggles to free him and then carries the cubs, one by one, across a jumble of jagged ice.

The mother finds a great split in the ice where they can plunge into the frigid water. *SPLOOSH!* The cubs paddle with their webbed front paws. *Rarfrarf. FWAP!* Three giant walruses smack their flippers on the water. Quickly the mother shows the cubs how to steer away with their back feet.

Finally she finds a place to come ashore. The cubs want to nap, but the mother nudges them awake until they shake hard and roll in the snow to dry off. Their fur cannot protect them unless it is clean and dry.

The cubs are stuck on land in August. They are still nursing, but there is not much else to eat. Then the cubs spot a lemming. They charge. The lemming darts into a tunnel. The mother shows the cubs how to dig and pounce. *Gulp!* Her two-ounce bite of lemming is only a tidbit for a bear that can devour 150 pounds at one meal. And now they are overheated. They swim in the ocean to cool off, and the mother shows them where to dive for a snack of kelp.

The ice bears are losing weight and try to save energy with a long sleep. *Cheepcheep chirp!* All around them baby birds hatch just when there is plenty for birds to eat. Some chicks probe the mud for insect larvae. Others eat seeds or snap at the clouds of mosquitoes. Half of the mosquitoes drink plant nectar to survive, but the females need blood to make their eggs. The cubs slap, slap, slap at mosquitoes that bite around their eyes. The mother digs a den down to the permafrost to escape the pests.

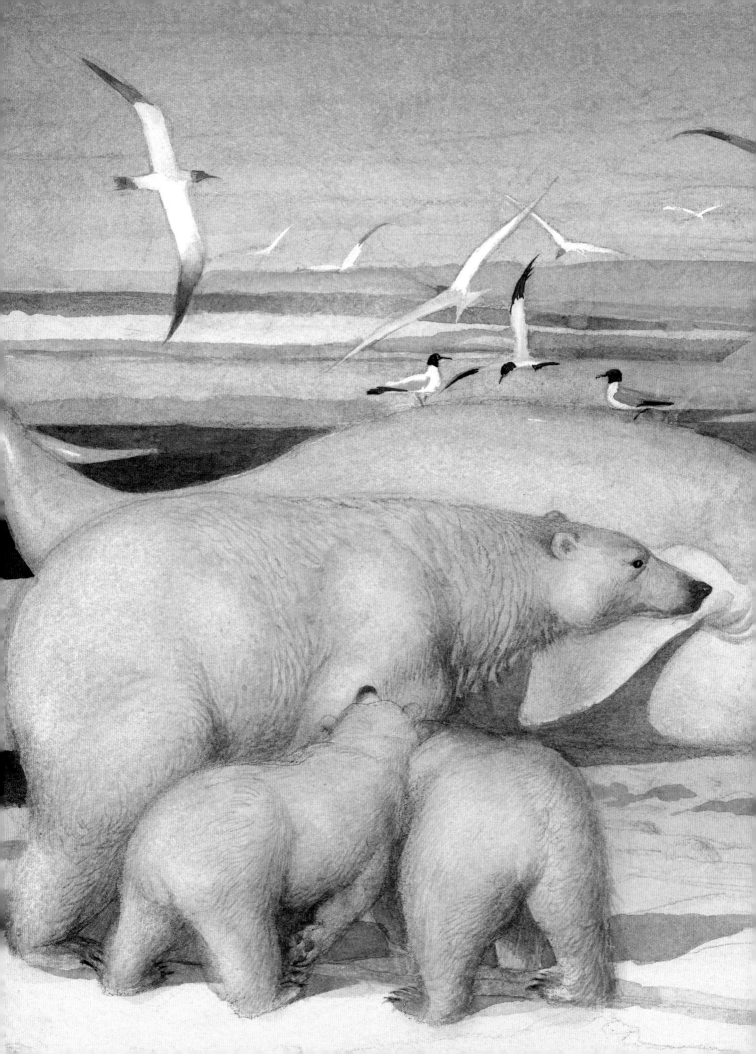

Snuffsniiiiif! The mother catches a whiff of dead whale, and the family follows the scent along the windy coastline. It's too blustery for mosquitoes. Polar bears come from all directions to gather around the beached beluga whale. The mother rubs noses with a large bear and waits for a share. Foxes, ravens, and gulls show up, too. The mother and her cubs do not get much.

In the short autumn, the bears find berries and cotton grass but they are getting bone-thin. They are waiting— waiting for the ocean to freeze.

After two more weeks of balmy weather, the temperature plunges quickly and snowflakes fall.

Honk! Honk! Kree! Flocks of birds fly south. Lemmings look for deep snow where they can dig their tunnels. And the bears pace back and forth until at last the ocean freezes.

Finally the ice bears can return to the ice, ready to fatten up on seals during the long cold winter ahead.

ARCTIC ICE REPORT

Warning! Warning! The earth is warming up and a million square miles of arctic sea ice have recently melted. Ice bears need ice to survive. They use the frozen ocean as a hunting platform to find seals, their main food. When the ice melts, the bears are stuck on land with little to eat. Some bears starve. Some drown trying to swim great distances across iceless seas. Some mother bears are too thin to raise triplets, twins, or even a single cub. Some dens slump and collapse before the cubs are old enough to be outside.

Double Alert! Seals need ice, too. They make dens on the ice to raise their pups. They swim below the ice to find arctic cod, a fish that requires ice. Walruses and whales, arctic foxes and sea birds also depend on ice. Caribou can drown if frozen streams on their migration routes thaw too soon.

Action Needed! If we don't take action soon, ice bears will lose their habitat and face extinction, along with many other creatures of the icy poles. But people can help save them. By burning less fossil fuel, humans can slow down the ice melt. We can also support organizations working to protect the arctic ecosystem and the animals and plants that live there.

Here are some organizations that are working to help the environment:

Audubon: www.audubon.org

Defenders of Wildlife: www.defenders.org

Environmental Defense: www.environmentaldefense.org

Lick Global Warming: www.lickglobalwarming.org

National Environmental Trust: www.net.org

National Wildlife Federation: www.nwf.org

Natural Resources Defense Council: www.nrdc.org

Nature Canada: www.naturecanada.ca

Ocean Conservancy: www.oceanconservancy.org

Physicians for Social Responsibility: www.psr.org

Polar Bear SOS: www.polarbearsos.org
   (created by the Natural Resources Defense Council)

Project Thin Ice: www.projectthinice.org
   (created by Greenpeace)

Save Our Environment: www.saveourenvironment.org

Sierra Club: www.sierraclub.org

Union of Concerned Scientists: www.ucsusa.org

U.S. Fish and Wildlife Service: www.fws.gov

Wilderness Society: www.wilderness.org

Wildlife Conservation Society: www.wcs.org

World Wildlife Fund: www.worldwildlife.org